The Death of Francis Bacon

Grief Is the Thing with Feathers
Lanny

Max Porter

The Death of Francis Bacon

faber

First published in 2021
by Faber & Faber Ltd,
Bloomsbury House,
74–77 Great Russell Street,
London WC1B 3DA

Typeset by Faber & Faber Ltd
Printed and bound by CPI Group (UK) Ltd, Croydon, CR0 4YY

Two John Berger quotations in section 1 are from
Portraits: John Berger on Artists,
edited by Tom Overton, Verso, London, 2015.

A CIP record for this book
is available from the British Library

ISBN 978–0–571–36651–4

2 4 6 8 10 9 7 5 3 1

Preparatory Sketch

Non-existent, pencil on paper, 6 x 4 in.

Did I draw this?

Frame or bed, hole could be window, flesh could
be flat, nobody looking,

        one body prostrate,
                        another attending.

Note to self but never did anything with it.
Promise me you'll hide this.

The body on the bed pinned down by sickness.

The body of the carer,   choices.
The body of the painting,   reckoning.

Madrid.
Unfinished.
Man Dying.

One

Oil on canvas, 60 x 46½ in.

Take a seat why don't you.

Hopeless angle, chin stuck on like a dumpling,
cheek like a chop, but I like the cut white sail of
the cap and the forearm border with the starched
guillotine sleeve.
This is all worth a look.

Take a seat why don't you.
I heard you before, piggy.

Run along fuet, poor sibling to the Catalan whip
on the bowl of peas with the garlic oil.
Darling mama, sister oh Dios, Mercedes, my hair
must be utterly laughable.

No oil.

She pats my little linen hill belly.

Hungry, starch and starve, all your thoughts of food and fizz.

The martyr Edward or the painter Francis?

She turns and that suddenly *is* a handsome prospect, twisted neck, thick line of brown shadow, that's what I'd seen this morning, nag-at-me ridge-bone, rather unholy, little bull at the door beneath a broken nose. I'd love to see her snarl. There's an odd lidded familiarity and the sense of too many teeth, teeth going all the way back down the throat, that's why she has to sit like that, as if sitting for me, lest those rows of teeth burp out.
I'd love to see you snarl.

Sí.

Minotauromaquia.
Sí sí.

My hair must be utterly laughable, I can feel it
fluffing, puffy, all the air I no longer have is up in
my hair. No oil.
Fuzz. Fuss. Fizz you say. Lust.

Stop now. Listen. So vain.

I ask her for Francis, and I say Please.
She takes from her face a handsome hardback
and breaks it open like it was made of crackling,
lacquered, and we are in the details and she licks
her finger, she licks the cut ridge of the pink tip
and sucks licks pits puts her finger in the middle
fingering rings an awkward van Dyck tapering
chub bell with the ring pinning the trimmed
figure to the belted indentation, bothers me,
paying attention, too pale.

Sister Are you in pain?
Francis Just working. Unbother that dangling
finger with a rag.

(What you know is that a seventeenth-century finger will say to a twentieth-century eye: Look at this, this little wooden box, if I put myself against the lid and push, see how tightly it makes its patient progress into that groove, heavens yes, it's perfectly tantalising, and you hardly need me to tell you with a found image what it's like.)

Slices her finger and holds open the cut to show me but I'm asleep and refusing to dance her little clichéd blood-dance so she reads:

Bacon is a very remarkable but not finally important painter.

BORING. I know this. I know what you're doing. She's up on the ceiling, in some kind of trapeze swing seat or harness, matte batwings, couldn't reach her if I tried.

These paintings are haunting because Bacon is a brilliant stage manager rather than an original artist; and because their emotion is concentratedly and desperately private.

Oh naff off you skag. Rien de tel que privé.

And the little policeman runs up to the camera and is about to scream, but the image is paused and down she comes from the ceiling above the bed and holds my eyelid open and says *not finally important*, and as the little policeman runs again to the camera and seems about to scream, it's paused again and she drops back down, again, like a great broken apparatus of tarpaulin and picnic stools and lifts my eyelid – it clicks as it leaves the eyeball – and says *desperately private*, and there he is, again, the pre-scream, the about-to-scream policeman with his little hat and I know exactly what this is, I know it step by step, it is arriving at a party, again, and feeling horribly new, unknown, lonely and awkward, affecting

disinterest and realising the only way is to spin
on in, whip up some energy, and for that we need
drinks and for that we need more drinks and she
lifts my eyelid again and says I will see you later,
dear boy.
Sí.

Intenta descansar.

Two

Oil on canvas, 65½ x 56 in.

Take a seat why don't you, but I'm still asleep so
she doesn't hear. Nice familiar weight at the foot
of the bed, the sort of fever guest weight, aunt
or mother, nurse, or the after-fuck check-up, to
tuck me in, still a little whiff of hurt in the room,
of procedures. Rather wonderful actually, to
be reminded of childhood sickness and post-
coital exhaustion in the same second. Rather
comforting. Close.

Take a seat why don't you.

I heard you before, piggy.

Process. Grouse. A throwaway remark to a
journalist. Twee my bloody tombstone.
Quail, redcurrant jus. Oysters. The pheasant stew
I tried to do after we had it at the claustrophobic
place. When I bit down on shot.

It's extraordinarily nice not to have to order or
get up, it all just arrives when I think of it and
somewhat offsets the embarrassment of Capelo,
lying a mile from here when I suppose I always
thought one might be murdered, have one's
throat slit, or be garrotted in an alley off Frith
Street.

Not comic, vultures. Bit down on shot and
regretted saying anything about accidents, I
can still feel it, right through me, like a shock.
Metal drill in my fillings right down through my
urethra. Buzzing in my underbladder.

Edward the Martyr or Francis the painter?

Oh hello ducky. You look like a pastry, a slightly
overdone bun. I would have you twisting to look
over your shoulder, cap on, uniformed, slight
formless gash where your crowded mouth is,
that lovely brow like a minotaur's shoulder in
the middle. Good face. Do you know the poem

Picasso wrote about Guernica? I was terribly, terribly struck by it, cries of children, cries of women, cries of birds, do you know it? He says, I think, something like, cries of the stew in the pot, can you imagine? Scorched earth and little button mushrooms, thyme, shallots, Manzanilla, I suppose, something dry, all sticky in the Le Creuset, I say bloody bring it out here, don't bother plating it up we'll eat from the casserole won't we darling, just bread, and more wine, I think that will do splendidly, look at that. May all who see thee bless the great creator who made so fair a thing, quite right! Quite right! Santé.

Edward was riding – OH DO FUCK OFF.
Edward was riding – YOU NASTY SINISTER MEAN-SPIRITED HAG.
Edward was riding – OH FINE.

Edward was riding up the hill.

Sister Listening?

Francis (*Broncoespasmo*) Wheeze. Please believe me, I'm not always like this. Lower me, raise me, give me more air, take away that ghastly blue pleather chair. (*Sleeping*)

Edward was chafing, long ride from Salisbury, slept on a bale, barely a hair on his bollocks, none on his chin and his arms ached, saddle sore on his left arse cheek, blister on his thumb, shoulders and neck stiff from the ride, cross and anxious hot young king, sweat in his eye stinging, unease in his belly, alarm bells ringing, just a boy, would he like a drink of course he'd like a drink, he's ridden from Salisbury, hawk, scabbard, leather flap, taste of chalk and whey, starving hungry but shite like gruel loose and feverish cramping a bit, nervous to eat, keen to sleep, here she is, the woman he fears in his future and fucks in his dreams, the sow on the hill, but she has a glass of beer and she hands it up and he feels a surge of hold me, bathe me, dry my hair, wipe my arse,

drain me, empty my balls into your downturned
mouth and let me sleep in your bed.

Sister ¿Estás bien?
Francis Sí, sí, thank you darling, just slightly
tight in my chest. Carry on.

And various pleasantries are exchanged, you
look well Aelfryth, you look well Edward, long
ride, good day, strong wind, sea air, here, some
beer, a long gladdening gulp of gold, the colour
of the stone, strange look, first cold, extremely
cold and makes him think of river swims and
soiling his sheets, shock, shame, the wet sock
game, being stabbed is the same, extraordinary
pain, the colour blue, lapis right through him,
and then again and again and she's walking
back into the castle and he's dripping venison
memory, white fat and clicking, smoke,
dripping onto the stones, trying to turn and
see where the hurt is, caught in the stirrup and
upside down, crack on the skull metal thump

19

in the side in a brawl with the pages, again, crack again, black, bits of his brain scattered on the track thumping down the hill down the hill down the hill and into the river Corfe, last thought is of the beer, wasted, where is the cup, we are concerned with those who notice the cup, yes the dead king, yes politics, meat and temporality, but also the well-made cup, perched body ripe and crucial on the road.

Yes. Now you've got me thinking. Unseated picador, all horse and no animal. Not good enough. This is how I think when I'm at it.

Thrown rider.

Horribly kitsch and pointless picture. Futile nod to decoration. But I do like the grey area. Feels like scab.

Several hundred quid in a pewter pint mug, light-catching cameo from a William Nicholson, behind the orange male nude I left half done. London is several days away in either direction.

A gold bit, chomp on, something to hold, teeth

on metal, imagine that, I used to like the idea of a back strap.

Yes, peeling a scab. Lifting off the whole clotty lot of it and seeing the root. Verruca stippled.

These are a few of my favourite things.

Yes, sister, that's just marvellous, you are quite marvellous. I thought it was Peter, reading to me, but I see of course it's you. I wonder if I might have no pain. If you'd be so kind.

No pain?

Sí, no pain.

Sí. Intenta descansar.

Three
Oil on canvas, 65 x 56 in.

Take a seat why don't you. Deakin? Thought
I smelt a friend of mine. Acqua di Colonia,
peppermint.

Sister Is chewing gum, piggy.
Francis I can't breathe especially well if truth be
told.

Julius Caesar or the painter Francis Bacon?

She can't hear me, I'm asleep. So drunk I conked
out in the cab and I said to him, How long have I
been asleep? Broad daylight. Sickening light.
How long have I been asleep? Excuse me, how
long have I been asleep? The meter was running,
at seven hundred quid, from Islington, for god's
sake man, did I sleep all day? And he turned
around and it was Deakin, but he couldn't speak
because he had a human fist in his mouth, trotter,

knuckles spilling out, teeth marks on dead skin.
John was clearly suffocating, his eyes were wide
in panic and I said Fucking hell old chap spit
it out, spit it out, and he grunted, Uh cuhhn
hrreeere Uh cuuhhnn hreee
What's he saying?

Sister Shhhh.
Francis Some of us are trying to speak.

The fist interrupts with a wet shplonk like a
dollop thud onto the canvas and leaves a stain,
deft impression, dent in the wet racing green,
rather good actually, shut up a second, gives
some doggy movement to the great waste of
her face, rather good actually, canine, to have
something scampering, something squirming,
so I wrung it out in a bucket, the saturated fist,
and used it like a cloth, swab, rubbed it back and
forth against the nice clean flesh of the breast
and the whole shape of the thing was suddenly
terribly clear, brilliant, all it needed was some

movement, bloody clumsy working from the photo, hiding, peeking, and the fist wobbling off like a tumour, voila. *Now* the green makes sense. Sorry if I'm repeating myself. I wonder if I could peel that neck of yours off and start again.

Julius Caesar?

Please. I'm going to save my breath, if you don't mind, dear.

Brutus sits at this desk, clutching a severed hand, which behaves.

He opens the fingers and rests his hot forehead in the palm, and it fits like a campaign, like a chore. He has a golden bowl to shit in, he has lamb and good wine, he has a canvas womb in which to toss and turn. No helmet or hood fits his head as well as the dead slave's hand.

History.

Cough. Ahem.

He doesn't look up—

27

How clever you are. Scholarship! The Haunting of Brutus from the marvellous children's book of ghost stories I found in Oxfam on the Gloucester Road. Yes, 'He doesn't look up.'

I'll take over. Let me. In comes the ghost of Caesar, yes, and Marcus Brutus gets the fright of his life, flashback to stabbed Caesar, folds of white, purple rim, yew, marble, cross-hatch dark arm hair, correct me if I'm wrong dear girl, then the same traumatic memory but a different shot of it, quite brilliant angle of the body as if we are lying on a tilted mezzanine, more blood, in black, good foreshortened spill, eyes open, and in comes the dead senator, robed man with puncture wounds and I can and will use that, folds, muscle, slightly you-know-who in the chin, which is why it alarmed me, self-portrait as ghost of Caesar, as royal baby, but then I lost the bloody thing. Some git nicked it from the studio. One of these shits who will write a god-awful hack-tosh-hagiography of me after I'm gone. Oh he was so scabrous, the monstrous pitiable Bacon, up at the bar, buying us drinks.

The figure pulled the robe aside and revealed a
body running and glistening with blood.

That's it sweetheart. Exactly. I thought I might
do a lot with that, and of course me being me
I'm clutching a ripped-out portrait of little
Don Carlos in one hand, and I can't resist an
unholy facial marriage, a quotation of sorts,
and therefore suddenly, brilliantly, pinned for
your eyes only, the Infante's chin is kissing the
punctured Roman's chest. I folded the head
over at the eyes and laid it on the injury. You
understand me. How I make these pictures work.

Listen, piggy, my turn.
Empty room, little bell ringing, which is the bell
the Infante has on the little royal waist. A shrill
yapping from the puppy. The bell rings because
you would never have had the courage to paint
such a person. You pick up the book, you rip out

the image, you borrow the chair, the arm, her
weight on the floor, and then you run away for
twenty years.

Don't be unkind.

Look, rich piggy. I look at you and you say yes
master, yes market, one more walk to the Prado,
one more glass of bubbles, but my face does not
move one millimetre, not even disdain, I don't
need to flinch, you are just any old executioner.

Yes, yes, now you're talking. I don't even turn
around. Head resting on the dead palm, I know
it's Caesar, or the king, or George, or Felipe,
knock knock a nice ripe face on the chopping
block for Mister Bake On, ready whenever you
are, begging eternal life if you please, come all
the way down, all the bloody way down, no need
to look, it's the same picture again, the little girl
dying at one hundred miles an hour, head lolling
on the velvet chair, don't need you here, have

everything I need, no point you staying old boy,
tell Willy to leave them in the hall. Tell everyone
to leave.

Sister Slow down. Breathe.
Francis Leave the photos on the floor and fuck
off! I want to be alone.

Great thumping load of brass and timpani falling
off the wall crashing onto a major chord:

He knew what had to be done.

He gripped the hilt of his sword and turned the
point against his stomach.

Sí. Okay.
Intenta descansar.

Four

Oil on canvas, 14 x 12 in.

Take a seat why don't you?
Are we rolling?
Will you take out any really daft bits?

It's an attempt to get at the sense of what is
looming up behind the person being hurt.

It's an attempt to keep the breast meat of the
bird moist while the skin is crispy.

It's an attempt to express my feelings about a
painter I have had a long unfashionable fixation
with.

It's an attempt to get art history out of the way
and let the paintings speak.

It's an attempt to hold catastrophe still so you
can get a proper sniff at it.

(*The artist rolls his hand as if curtseying in the old
fashion.*)

I see it as a fact or thing, surrounded by other facts or things, from the world of facts or things and I refuse to say any more until . . .

(*The artist twists on the sofa. Fidgets. Pats his pockets. Gets up. Finds packet.*)

. . . Until I've found my blasted ciggies!

(*Canned laughter*)

Mussolini or Bacon?

Go, go, we're up and running now, let's talk until lunch. Bacon! Let's have it.

He is fundamentally a colourist, in the childish sense. He draws his simple pictures and he colours them in. At his most sophisticated he has been granted stickers:
Red arrows,
Bulbs,

Wounds, cricket pads, little bits of lonely
nonsense architecture.
He has fun sticking these flat gimmicks on his
fake figures, or behind them.
Sometimes he sets aside his juvenile addictions
long enough to look hard at a face or ponder
patiently a colour field, and these are cheap
trick successes, related to Heal's, Habitat, *Home
Interiors Magazine* more than to the great
painters he slavishly imitates.

Sister, you're giving me a terrible desire to punch
something.

He treats his heroes as he treats a scientific
magazine or a porno, or a student's guide to
Western Art, just a glance, a cut, a rip, a borrow,
then binned, denied, questioned with no ear
for reply, and it is tiring, year after year, Bacon's
baby struggles with his own limitations, it is
exhausting to behold such huge quantities of
paint being wasted.

Enough!

Sister Hurting?
Francis Almost. Go on. A little more.

His distortions are not snobbery, or innovation,
they are lies. He is a flamboyant and brilliant liar
who got lucky and found his medium.

At first he worried me with fear
I was timid, scared and young
My shoulders were too rounded
To bear his cat-rough tongue

The purple, the orange, the shocking pink, the
great lilac mistake, the poor man got so used
to seeing his huge paintings in huge galleries,
pumped up with huge space, huge palettes, huge
cheques, he egged himself on to absolute banality,
temper tantrums that he can't actually make a
figure move, and then his best pictures looked
familiar, and fetched a pretty penny, because they

38

were copies of his earlier worst, his sturdier work,
his curdling burst of fifties kitsch, his own podgy
face trademarked, pretending it confronted death
when all it did was illustrate again and again a
lazy fear of it.

And then he promised me sleep
I was brazen, fat and old
My hand was shaking all day long
His salty seed was cold.

Here is a bespoke interview style, three bottles,
three courses, tempt me down the garden path,
gossip about my friends, slander the Americans,
bravo hard heart, you treat, you card.

In the end he is the great skiver, oil paint his lame
accomplice, the marketplace his grim enabler.

Baby fear of it?

Baby fear of it.

Do I seem babyish? Frightened?
Sylvester was always very good at making me
feel that what I was saying was interesting. You
might indulge me in that regard. You might let
me smoke a while, and steer me back to mouths
or openings, popes or noticing. No?

Enfermera.

Arrow in the thigh, 'kitsch'; arrow in the belly,
'banal'; one right through the neck, gasping for
breath, gargling blood, 'slavishly imitating'; argh,
my dear, can't you see I'm dying here, thwump,
straight to the heart, 'illustration'; there's no
recovery, the vital organ, the martyr Francis tilts
his rubber jaw to heaven and dies, spurts the
viewer with cum and vermilion.

Hermana?

Sister?

Sí. There is nothing here of any value. We try again. As you teach me.

Intenta descansar.

Five

Oil on canvas, 78 x 58 in.

Take a seat why don't you?

Perhaps lean back into the swan, à la contorted boy into falling drapery. Now, because I like you, this will be difficult.

I'm going to tip you forward out of the frame and whip your buttock with lead white to give a sense of fight.

You're going to be a person spilling out of a trap, and I'm going to be a person who is fatherly, fuckable, and this is going to upset you, exhilarate me and interest scholars.

I'm this person, pinned to the wall.

Saskia. Hitching up her undergarments. A fag butt on the shit sheen of the Serpentine.

You – telling everyone again and again how spontaneous you are, as if the whole golden

edifice crumbles if they find out you've done
some drawings.
You – saying 'Friends are thieves of time' again
and again until you have none.

Yes, bresaola, radish, parmigiana, the little
Italian place, eating whatever I wanted, ordering
for myself, not trying to charm anyone, me,
impervious to charm, myself, but seeing him
in the reflection and being utterly delighted to
discover I am smiling.

I am smile. Venus and Cupid.
Anyone but Bacon who sold himself to bankers
like all good painters before him, but found
himself alone, unable to breathe, in Madrid.

A stained bump of damp plaster on the ceiling
becomes a face, becomes a chubby putto,
becomes the oversized child I fancifully yearned
to care for, becomes hands and feet sucked
free, pinkly modelled in the room and dribble

dripping onto my waxy almost death mask and
down, down, lands on me softly, pulls down
the sheet, so hungry, hurry yanking, questing,
opening my pyjamas and searching for the nipple,
upside-down angle Veronese staged or trompe
l'œil, the baby on strings is the baby on a different
plane, language, the dying painter is scarcely
an image, never the two shall meet except to
feed, latched on, glugging, sucking, me flat and
mathematical like Mantegna's Dead Christ, the
feeding child rampant on the diagonal then gone.

Just an ochre blob on the ceiling of room 417,
Clínica Ruber.

Is he gone? Blanco?

Sí.

It's done, then. I gave them an awful lot of money.
Would have liked to ride on my bicycle with my
big brother Harley.

The painter Francis Bacon or the corpse
Mussolini? (Do you think you are the loneliest
man in the world?)

Can't you say, instead, Your father or horses? And
I would reply quick as a flash, Oh horses, I never
spare my father a thought, but I think of horses
often. I invented things to make the interviews
interesting, and sometimes, as I said them, I
realised they were true, intoxicating ways to think
oneself into shape, very much like painting.
Anyway, anything but Bacon, por favor. Torment.
I am ever so sick of myself.

Close your eyes, we will now paint, together,
this expensive scandalous canvas and you can
prepare your lies (I didn't think I just made, it
was unforeseen, painting is being handed things,
I don't know where ideas come from, compelled
by inner storms to dollop a swastika on), poor
muse-stuck bubble-dweller, budge over, six foot
square, herringbone, tight and ready, room for

the two of us, the two of them.

Subject.

You can't stop thinking about that photo, you've
thought about it for years, Mussolini and Petacci,
posed embrace, broken faces, her little row of
teeth, his great rubberised lake of violence, the
human face punished to formless.

I think we have them smack bang in the middle
on the circular bed (which is your pout).
I think we have a receding diagonal frame, with
the upside-down corpses, put there for their own
compositional protection.

Green metre squared. Thick, weirdly stubborn
colour. Obstreperous. A 7 p.m. colour. A two-
men-talking-in-the-study colour. Easy drinkable
claret and someone senior gripping my wrist
colour. Hate to admit it, English colour.

Green against cream.
Racing green, dated green, belatedly I worked

49

out how to dilute the paste and fill the cut-circle space with it: green.

Green baize, and a cross, and a rose. They litter the foreground and gather pace with the sense everyone ought to bugger off while I'm making a good/bad picture, this one is becoming extremely good/bad, won't eat for a while, smoke two packs of ciggies and get this right, little bits of could be bone, little folds of could be mouth, little curl of could be tenderness, sleepwalking into this.

Crowd versus body, these two dead animals, we will need a very clean world to set these two copulating heaps of flesh upon. Hooks perhaps, or beige.

Show me nature.

I can't. I'm the least green painter in the history of marks.

(cheat)

Show me how this mess steps aside and lets you
make a perfect surface of unbroken colour.

It's not for watching.

(lie)

I'm asleep. Find me a painter alive today who can
do what I can do in the time I can do it, no help.
Alone.

Sí. Intenta descansar.

Six

Oil on canvas, 37 x 29 in.

Take a seat wh

                y don't you?rattdpissed as a afrt

Siddow
   nstand upBackto me. Great long
gdrooping fagash, fooping drag ashnever
know what hethinking. Whatsehithiking. Perfect
   arse run bead a
spiton run bead glob

        into hn and one fingerup knuckle deep and

                        slappingthumb f

            uckinghim holding his
cheek corner of my eyeon

                Eye on the picture,

passis
pass his cig back aroundandstarts
wankinghishimself

            mightbesick start wallp
wallopsd fingfuckerng him

            punch hard

gruning

      hmmff

55

sitback on me armunder and
grbahis balls grb his

                balls take a seat whydonbtyou
take a seat whyd ohntyou

Francis Bacon or Caravaggio?

Wait. Same set of images, sparkling sober, fresh
out of the shower, ready to work.
His back to me, George, playing at being
angry, clutching his cigarette, I know what he's
thinking, undo belt, pull down trousers, reach
around and out springs his hardon, briskly sets
to wanking, he reaches back around and holds
the filter and I take a long sucking drag on his
fag, reaching for it like a feeding animal, and he
puts one foot forward slightly, lifts his arse and
I spit on my fingers and work one in, George
grunts, palm up-as-a-cup middle finger fucking
him to the knuckle as hard as I can and he drops
the cigarette butt, reaches round and grabs
my hair, too rough, I pull my finger out with

a wet clack and slap his hand away, shove him,
stupid oaf, dropping a lit cigarette in the studio,
fucking imbecile, and he moans and empties two
tablespoons of himself into his hand.

Francis Bacon or Caravaggio?

Wait. Same set of images, ten years later, three
six-foot canvases, you are a

strong

Sister Tacky
Francis Elastic

man

got me held here, like this, je suis un pédéraste,
less, turn around a bit, tu es un souvenir, wrestler
on the sprung boards, can't really work out

whether to put a nice navy blue behind, him
out there, me in here, scared of each other, him
in front, playing to the gallery, and me biting
down on my shirt collar, pain like a stabbing in
my kidneys, nothing elegiac or profound just I
would've given you a key you daft sod, I would've
given you a key you silly bugger, I'm crying all
over my supper, I would have tilted you forward
out of the middle panel and out into the lap of
the beholder, you could have used a key, you silly
daft soft toy . . .

. . . meet you in the gift shop, tray English, canvas
tote, Freud on a napkin, Bacon cashmere throttle
the nanny, Spanish Annie.

Sister Tacky
Francis Plastic

Caravaggio or Bacon?
Caravaggio please, but three, and hung high, and
walking left to right, keeping the middle still.

Barge any old farts out of the way, I'm a fucking
artist and I'm trying to tell a story.

One: How to represent a leaden headache that
has plagued him from Napoli up to Porto Ercole,
easy peasy, lift his cranium off, fold pink brain
outwards and smear it on the greasy hair, one eye
socket hacked open with a sharp object – germy
– the other inert, fallow-deer-dead, hiding from
the sun, which offends him, suggest bone where
nose was, suggest smirking guilty grimace of
poisoned pain that would kill him, leave actual
paint on his cause of death, actual paint in his
actual bloodstream.

Two: Wounds. Typical of me, all the gore, special
effects, now I am the empty-head celebrity
meat master of macabre, lead in his wounds,
champagne, doomed. Sticky, smells like turpfish,
curdled cheese burps, trying to hold this still, just
ill red holes in the dark, weeping, but there's a
sense of still-living in the pink, despite the static

59

sarsen weight of it, sunburnt Roman waiting to
die in the Tuscan night, why not fleck the lip of
the . . .

(Is the patient with you? Keep still please, while
we're in the middle image. Can you hold the
phone to his ear, Caravaggio, tick, definitely him
he has distinctive death rattle, abdominal pain,
cramps and vomiting, tick, discoloration of the
urine and faeces, tick.)

. . . foul-smelling injury to make it shine, make-
up, still wet when the chatty boys from the
Marlborough came to pick up. Take me while I'm
wet, prendimi signore, sell me quick, I am merely
the middle. Expensive cologne to cover it up.
Hate myself.

Three: Rolling over into the sheer textual left
to right the line between his work and mine,
several centuries of light on human flesh, real
people in oil, roiling with the worst moods and

most painful injuries and hyperbolic self-pitying
praise-hungry mania to ever afflict a genius
with a brush and a fight-me flush. I'm not happy.
Paying actors. Posing. Less and less surprised by
light.

I want him leaving. I want the eye to trundle off
past him. I'm inside the bloody thing watching
you regard it, late sixties, hearing you say it's the
best work I've done.

Back around to the left, glancing off the face of
the person in pain, as if the mouth is the habit
the eye has to kick. I'm inside the bloody thing
watching you regard it, early eighties, hearing you
say it's the worst work I've done.

No, not this time. I want you lost, lover and critic
kicked off the gum jetty at the end of the triptych
licked or on your knees, back to me saying Please,
I did it to hurt you, to spoil Paris, and me saying
CAN'T HEAR YOU, I did it because it was easy,

your profile, cut out, ready, and everyone else was dying and I had a horrid stabbing realistic knack of surviving. Endless errors, no confusion, gag me, stop me speaking thinking about you, stop me working.
One two three. Nothing but pain.

Sí.

I'm die-ready.

Sí. Soon, piggy.
Intenta descansar.

Seven

Oil on canvas, 77 x 52 in.

Take a seat why don't you.

Cheek.

I still feel ill.

I know, love.

I've been a bit lost.

I know, love. Shall we let some women in?

Muriel, *have mercy on me, barefoot that I go*,
punching herself again and again, odalisque
made of lamb cutlets, shuck her out onto the
tabletop, saddle her, into a sort of funereal
Princess Margaret, crop and jodhpur shrew,
mutant kangaroo, get a better look at you.

I remember being shoved up against the ripe
armpit of my cousin, sardines in a cupboard in
Dublin, holding our breath, and I rolled over and
reached for something to hold, found a doorknob
and held, I was like Diana with no bow, inhaling
my Pamela, blissful, and then Boo, Ianthe,
Germany, no mama, nurses, teachers, Isabel,
Winifred's rings of flesh like Del Piombo, bracelet,
chub, Michelin man sheen in the fever.

Immaculate studio. Not much money.
Six hundred paintings.
Messy studio. Plenty of money.
Lunch at Long Melford. Scarred on the body and
lonely.
So do, nightingale, sing full merry,
Bitter chest. Sad old gentleman making bad
work, limited vision, shallow as a plate (and other
stolen idioms).

The century abandoned me at dusk.

I panicked and added more newsprint.
Crappy friends leaving me,
crappy artists, crappy bitter aphorisms pouring
out of me,
plasticky surgery belches,
dapper, bandaged, trashed,
honestly I behaved horribly.

I've been lost a bit. It's just dying, finally.
Pity me, *up and lead the dance of fate.*

Choose now.
'Greatest Living Painter' Francis Bacon Breathes
His Last in Madrid, 1992, or The Violent Death of
the Painter Francis Bacon, London, 1979?

Ducky thank you, you're lovely to me, I'm sure I
don't deserve it, melliloquent sister. The fun one,
please. Seventy-nine, golly, yes please. Drink? Yes,
let's. What a gas. I'm ready.

Very well, press play.

The Violent Death of the Painter Francis Bacon,
London, 1979:

bm\tss, bm\tss, bm\tss, bm\tss.
The perfect time of day; the final dreamy evening.
bm\tss, bm\tss, bm\tss, bm\tss.
Extremely groovy feeling, no sex-sense spared.

(*God help us all he's cranked it up a notch.*)
Much laughter. Daftness. Cruel Afters.
Forty-one Dean Street, then heading a few doors
north, very noisy.
Crooks and lovers, after dinner to the French
House for dirtier wine.

Cut into the scene a suave tight-fitted Ganymede
clutching a brush, with a bit of rough on his
arm, stubble, musty, holds a cig like a shiv,
scabbed knuckles, nicked a silver plate from the
club, nipped to the bogs, came back pink and
grinning, perky pig, truffle hunter to the bar, to
the bar! Kneel like Mars to kiss the Venus in high

heels' chipolata toes and snaffle a fallen Dunhill.
¡Abrazo! Last night on earth.

Rim shot!
Francis? Still with us?
Yes, marvellous. Lightheaded, happy.

They surprised the painter Bacon and the mood
of the piece was authentically violent.

Bag over the head, Payne's grey middle of the night
on his way to piss, sure he didn't go to sleep alone,
punched until dizzy, bigoted insults, couple of
cracked ribs and some kidney torment, weeping,
winded, almost-nice pain, good to be in the dark
for once, down the stairs, into a van, fifteen-
minute drive to the river, bag off, knuckles dressed
in metal smash his nose and now he's fast asleep . . .

He's fast finale asleep.

He isn't waking up ever again.

Bits of tooth, cocaine blood and gristle in his whistle.

Calm and quiet, carnal quiet canal smell duck poo paving past caring but surprised.

Sister Honoured.
Francis Deeply humbled and grateful to be afforded such a bespoke ritual, it's very exciting.

Into a canvas coffin.
It's not the cough that carries you off . . .

Sister It's the coffin they carry you . . .
Francis (coughing) Sorry, spoilt it.

Into a canvas coffin, anthropoid box of beechwood, primed casket, stapled, measured to fit, no room to flap, room for one, a 3D palace for a furniture maker turned frame tamer, and in he went, grinning stupidly.

The last light. Famous painter's last rites.

In went turps. In went cadmium powder, bloody
mess, rags, two dozen unclean brushes, a comb,
tins, jars, a hundred winsors, a hundred newtons,
flannels, letrasets, an empty bottle of Krug, three
hundred quid in a greasy roll, a lighter, and then
they . . .

Pissed in the box.

Spat in the box.

Spunk, champagne, linseed oil, mixed in the
mind. Dashed, toothbrush-smeared and splashed
in the box.
Some legacy-delicate work, pentimenti, reaching
in and dabbing the palm of the hand with a
tiny black spot. Making sure an advert for oral
hygiene can be seen in the ripped innards of a
magazine.

He's gurgling like a bathtime baby, past present
gloopy future, MORE.

Struggling for breath, broncoespasmo, aire,
aire, lovely lads they know what they're doing,
professional lads, they chuck in arrows,
syringes,
table legs,
ligaments,
papers,
light fittings,
a red hand,
a sink, a bull,
all the props he's used to make a set-up pop.

Then sand.
Gallery-grade, kiln-dried, Perspex-cured, money-
no-object sand. Late Style.

Aire. Respirar. Please.

Then powder. Endless coloured powders, open

the reflex or gagging hungry idea of his mouth
and the pigment fills the throat, into the painter
Bacon's clogged bronchi, into his untidy lungs
and then they stand down, get back, see the
whole thing, because

his busy hands

have

finally stopped

fidgeting.

Blessed relief.

Que el Señor que te libera del pecado te salve y te
resucite.

Last sight isn't human after all, is pure throb
colour on the heart inside.

Get some distance, stand back, six feet, no glass,
no label, no price list, no body, no gallerist.

Just the painting.

Seal the lid. Is pure throb colour on the heart
inside.

No more.
Is pure throb colour on the heart inside.

Sí. Intenta descansar.